Careless wishes

Carole Wilkinson

Illustrated by Brian Harrison

KINGSCOURT / McGRAW-HILL

Careless Wishes
Copyright © 2001 Rigby Heinemann

Rigby is part of Harcourt Education, a division of
Reed International Books Australia Pty Ltd ABN 70 001 002 357.

Text by Carole Wilkinson
Illustrations by Brian Harrison
Designed by Andrew Cunningham

Published in the United Kingdom by Kingscourt/McGraw-Hill, a division of the MH Companies. All rights reserved. No part of this publication may be reproduced or distributed in any form or by any means, or stored in a database or retrieval system, without the prior written consent of Kingscourt/McGraw-Hill, including, but not limited to, network or other electronic storage or transmission, or broadcast for distance learning. Originally published in Australia by Rigby Heinemann, a division of Reed International Books Australia Pty Ltd.

KINGSCOURT/McGRAW-HILL

Shoppenhangers Road, Maidenhead
Berkshire, SL6 2QL
Telephone: 01628 502730
Fax: 01628 635895

www.kingscourt.co.uk
E-mail: enquiries@kingscourt.co.uk

Printed in Australia by Advance Press

10 9 8 7 6 5 4 3 2 1

ISBN: 0-07-710329-7

Contents

1 **Toil and Trouble** 1

2 **Bruised Skin** 11

3 **Only Birds Can Fly** 21

4 **Mixed Blessings** 33

5 **Shades of Pink** 41

6 **Too Many Women** 50

7 **A Little Piece of China** 61

8 **Feast for the Ancestors** 75

CHAPTER ONE

Toil and Trouble

MATILDA MABEL MAUD SHARP looked up at the early morning sky. It was streaked pink and grey, the same colours as the birds squawking overhead. Steam rose from the copper. Matilda was glad of the warmth from the fire. She grated a handful of yellow soap, threw it into the water and stirred it with the dolly stick, which was bleached white at one end from spending so much time in hot soapy water. Wash day. Matilda hated wash day.

Betsy was busy sorting the washing into four piles: the white linens, the delicate whites, the coloured things and the cleaning cloths.

2 Careless Wishes

"Are you going to stand there staring at the sky all day?" asked Betsy as she dumped the tablecloths into the water.

Matilda sighed and wished she didn't have to help with the washing every Monday. She poked the tablecloths down into the boiling water and stirred some more. She felt like an old witch at her cauldron. She was usually happy to be up and ready to start the day. Mondays were different.

"I'll go and strip the beds now," Betsy said.

There were just three of them in the house—Matilda, her Aunt Philadelphia and

Betsy their maid—but it took nearly a whole day to wash their things. On wash days, Matilda was pleased she didn't have a horde of brothers and sisters as some girls at school did.

Once the white linens were boiling and the collars and cuffs were soaking in a bucket, Matilda could think about breakfast. Betsy served Matilda porridge, a boiled egg and strong tea at the kitchen table, as she did every morning. Aunt Philadelphia liked to have her breakfast on a tray in her room. She didn't have to get up early on wash day to have her bed stripped. There were two sets of sheets for her bed. Her bedding was changed on Fridays.

Betsy didn't approve of breakfast in bed. She thought it was a bad habit for a Christian woman, even if she was reading Bible stories and pamphlets about missionaries in Africa. Not that she said that to Aunt Philadelphia, but she told Matilda often enough. Matilda didn't mind at all. If Aunt Philadelphia was up for breakfast, they'd have to eat it in the dining room. Matilda preferred the bright kitchen with the warmth from the kitchen range.

After breakfast, Matilda and Betsy scrubbed all the white collars and cuffs on the washboard to get rid of the grime and grease spots. Betsy poked at the copper with the dolly stick.

"They've stewed long enough," she said.

Matilda helped Betsy haul the heavy wet sheets out of the copper and put them through the mangle to squeeze out all the soapy water. Next came rinsing, adding blue, more mangling and then the collars and cuffs had to be starched. Then they hung the sheets on the line, being careful not to let the edges drag in the dirt, otherwise they'd have to start again.

The worst thing about wash day was that Matilda didn't go to school till midday. Misses Sarah and Ann Beasley, who ran the Wesleyan school, didn't like their students missing lessons, but they knew it couldn't be helped. Not every household could afford to have a laundry maid, and it was important for young ladies to learn about laundry.

Betsy sang all the time she worked. She didn't mind wash day at all.

"If you'd done the wash back at home, you wouldn't complain," she said every time Matilda grumbled about the work. "Back in England, I did the wash in all weathers, rain or snow. And, while it was stewing, I'd be up and down three flights of stairs carrying tea and hot water to the family. And the days when it was sunny enough to dry a whole wash, I could count on one hand. There'd be clammy wet things draped over everything inside."

Betsy thought Australia was a wonderful place. Plenty of sun to dry the washing, single-storey houses and a full eight months of the year when no fires needed to be lit. What more could you ask for?

Aunt Philadelphia thought it an unnatural place, full of birds that screeched instead of chirped and trees that never lost their leaves. And so much sun had to be bad for the health.

Matilda had never known any other place but Australia. She didn't like the sound of the grimy English cities or the cold winters. Betsy said if Matilda was in England, she wouldn't be allowed to wander around by herself. Matilda was glad she'd been born in Ballarat.

Aunt Philadelphia was a good woman. Everyone told Matilda that. She made stockings for the poor, sang hymns outside public houses on Saturday nights, packed and delivered food hampers to widows with children and helped raise money for the missionaries.

Charity was Aunt Philadelphia's life. The kindest thing she had done (so people said) was to take Matilda in when her father had been crushed to death in a mining accident. Matilda was only six when he died. She couldn't even remember her mother, who had died of consumption when Matilda was a baby.

Aunt Philadelphia had a small income from England and she sewed to earn a little extra money. This enabled her to run the house left to her by her brother and keep Betsy as a maid-of-all-work. Providing for Matilda was really beyond her means, but she didn't complain. She said having Matilda with her saved her the expense of employing a lady's companion. Aunt Philadelphia's charity work included regular visits to the orphanage, where she taught the girls good manners and respect for one's betters. Matilda was very grateful that she didn't have to live in that awful place and tried to help her aunt without grumbling.

When Matilda got home from school that afternoon, Betsy had a blanket spread on the kitchen table and was ironing the whites. Her face was red and sweating. The sheets and tablecloths were in neat piles and she was working on the aprons. She put the flat iron back on the range to heat up again.

"Can you bring in the coloureds and hang out the cleaning cloths?" she asked.

Matilda did as she was told. As she came back into the kitchen, Aunt Philadelphia swept in from the parlour.

"I'd like you to come with me to the greengrocer, Matilda," she said as she pinned on her bonnet. Aunt Philadelphia was the neatest person Matilda knew. Her lace trim was always white as snow, her boots shiny, her skirts never creased. Her hair was always in a neat bun.

Not a single hair dared to escape. Matilda had no idea how her aunt did it. She had only to step outside the front door to find her boots dusty, her cuffs grimy and her hair blowing about like ribbons on a maypole.

"But we go to the greengrocer's on Wednesdays," said Matilda. "Today's Monday."

"I know exactly what day it is, Matilda."

Each Wednesday, Aunt Philadelphia visited the butcher, the baker and the greengrocer to arrange the deliveries for the following week. Most people sent their servants to do this, but Aunt Philadelphia was a fussy shopper.

"We are entirely dependant on the food we eat, Matilda," her aunt was fond of saying. "If we want to be healthy of body and pure of mind, we must eat healthy and pure foods."

If she bought apples, she wanted them a particular size and shade of green. Meat had to have an exact proportion of fat. A loaf of bread had to be a certain height and not a millimetre more. Each week, she liked to discuss with the shopkeepers the size, colour and weight of everything that would end up on their table. This was the first time they had ever been to the greengrocer on a Monday.

"I'm not going for vegetables, Matilda," said Aunt Philadelphia as they walked briskly up Albert Street. Matilda always had trouble keeping up with her aunt's strides. She was too out of breath to ask questions and the purpose of their visit remained a mystery.

There were some fine buildings in Ballarat. Many of the shops were made of brick and stone. The houses were mainly wooden, but decorated with fancy woodwork on the gables and verandahs. Ballarat was not a pretty place though. The streets were dusty in summer and muddy in winter. Every patch of vacant ground had been dug up in the search for gold. There were holes and piles of slag everywhere. People were always in danger of falling down old mine shafts.

On the outskirts of town, there were makeshift camps of tents and rough huts, the machinery of working mines and the falling-down shacks of abandoned ones. Every tree had been chopped down to use as fuel or to build huts, houses and mining shafts. Matilda liked to walk, but it wasn't pleasant to walk outside town. That was why she loved the Botanical Gardens. It was always lovely and green, full of trees and ferns and fountains.

Their house in Albert Street was on the edge of the town right up against the gold diggings. Aunt Philadelphia liked their house because it was close to the Lydiard Street Wesleyan Church. Not so desirable was its closeness to the Chinese camp at Golden Point. Even though it was less than half-a-mile away, Matilda had never been there before. Not once. Ballarat children didn't even have to be told to stay away from it; they just knew it was a dangerous place.

CHAPTER TWO

Bruised Skin

THE GREENGROCER'S shop was in Bridge Street between the drapery and the ham-curer. It was almost a mile away, but Aunt Philadelphia enjoyed exercise even if it was along dusty unmade streets. Above the door, a painted sign read "Greengrocery, Sing Chow Mong, established 1860". The bell above the door rang as they entered. Inside, the smell of the place always gave Matilda a start. It was a foreign smell, impossible to describe.

The vegetables and fruit were arranged in neat piles. The apples all seemed to be the same size and colour, the lettuce heads were all open.

There were no bruises or wormholes on anything. That was why Aunt Philadelphia shopped there. Other greengrocers in town had their fruit in rough boxes and you had to pick through them to find the unblemished ones.

Sing Chow Mong was behind the counter weighing up quantities of herbs on a small set of scales. He wore a black gown that came down to his ankles and his black hair was tied back in a long thin plait. He put down his scales and bowed slightly to them.

Besides selling vegetables, Mr Chow Mong made herbal concoctions for sick Chinese people. It was the herbs that gave the shop its strange smell. Matilda had also heard that he stuck needles into people, which was supposed to cure certain illnesses.

Aunt Philadelphia inspected a pyramid of oranges until there were no other customers in the shop. Then she turned to the Chinese man.

"I have decided to try your treatment, Mr Chow Mong," she said.

Mr Chow Mong bowed again. Matilda looked at her aunt with surprise. She knew her aunt suffered greatly from pains in the arm brought on by the hours of fine sewing that she did each day. They had got so bad, she couldn't sleep at night.

Mr Chow Mong had noticed her discomfort on a previous visit and had told her he believed he could cure the pains.

"Would you care to step through here," he said, indicating a curtain. He spoke very good English.

Now Matilda understood why she had to accompany her aunt. It wouldn't have been proper for her to be treated by such a man if she was alone. Most people wouldn't have thought it proper anyway.

Behind the curtain was a small room that contained a cane chair, a table with flowers carved around the edges and a wooden bench.

"You aren't going to be stuck all over with needles are you, Aunt?" asked Matilda.

"No. Mr Chow Mong has another treatment in mind for me," her aunt replied.

The Chinese man entered the room with a swish of his gown.

"If you would please roll up the sleeve of your garment, Miss Sharp."

Without hesitation, Aunt Philadelphia undid the buttons on her right cuff and rolled up the sleeve of her dress past the elbow.

"If you would lay your arm on the table."

Aunt Philadelphia did as she was told.

Mr Chow Mong lit a small oil lamp and brought five glass spheres from a cupboard. They were like small round-bottomed jars, each with a hole at one end and a lip. He lit a long taper on the flame and placed it briefly inside one of the jars. He then quickly pressed the open end of the jar against the skin of Aunt Philadelphia's arm.

The jar fixed onto her arm, sucking her white flesh in a bulge inside it. He did the same with the other four jars until Aunt Philadelphia's lower arm was covered with them, each one sucking in part of her arm.

Aunt Philadelphia sat calmly as if this was a perfectly normal way to spend a Monday afternoon. After about ten minutes, Mr Chow Mong pulled off the jars. Aunt Philadelphia now had five circular marks on her arm. Two were faint pink rings, two were bright red patches, and one was an ugly purple blotch like a bruise, as if someone had struck her with a heavy object. Mr Chow Mong nodded with satisfaction.

"Here," he said, pointing to the ugly purple mark. "This is where the problem lies. I have freed the blockage of bad blood. Now I will mix you some herbs."

Aunt Philadelphia rolled down her sleeve.

Out in the shop, thankfully, there were no other customers to see them come out through the curtain. Only one old Chinese man came in wanting cabbage while Mr Chow Mong used his little scales to weigh out the special herbs for Aunt Philadelphia.

16   Careless Wishes

Mr Chow Mong's herbs were nothing like the herbs that Betsy put in soup. They looked like a collection of leaves, berries and bits of tree bark gathered by a child on a walk. He ground a piece of white rock in a bowl and added that to the mixture and wrapped it in a brown paper parcel.

"Boil these in three cups of water," Mr Chow Mong instructed. "Reduce the liquid to one cup, pour it off and boil twice more with two cups of water. Use a clay pot, not an iron one. Drink a cup of the liquid twice a day."

They didn't have a clay pot at home, but

Mr Chow Mong was happy to supply them with one. It was a strange looking thing with a spout sticking out of one side and a handle sticking out of the other. He wrapped it in brown paper and gave it to Matilda to carry.

Betsy was afraid of the Chinese pot.

"I'm not using that thing," she said, skirting around it as if it might jump up and bite her. "What's wrong with a good iron pot?"

She threatened to hand in her notice if she was forced to use foreign kitchenware. In the end, Matilda had to prepare the herbs. The boiling herbs gave off a strong, sweet smell with a hint of dirty stockings. Betsy ran outside with her apron over her nose and refused to come back in. Even Aunt Philadelphia went around the house sprinkling lavender water.

"You'll be poisoned if you drink that foul mixture," shouted Betsy from the back yard. "I wouldn't touch anything made by that man."

"Betsy, Mr Chow Mong is a herbalist, a knowledgeable man. There is no reason to have any fear of this remedy. The Chinese are God's people just the same as we are," said Aunt Philadelphia.

After the herbs had been boiled three times, Matilda strained the remaining liquid into a jug. It was a thick, brown soup with traces of the white powder and little pieces of leaf floating on the surface.

"Drink that stuff and who knows what diseases you'll catch," Betsy yelled from the wash house where she was sitting because it was getting dark and chilly outside.

Aunt Philadelphia poured out a cup of the warm liquid. Matilda thought her aunt might lose her nerve. But she held her nose and drank the foul stuff down in three gulps.

Betsy refused to come back into the kitchen that evening. Matilda had to prepare a meagre supper of bread, cold meat and cheese. She took some to Betsy who ate in the wash house.

Almost every evening, Aunt Philadelphia and Matilda sewed. Not the sort of sewing that other gentlewomen did—embroidery or lace making, for instance. Their sewing wasn't for amusement. Matilda had to be careful to keep it a secret. Aunt Philadelphia didn't think it was a shameful thing for a gentlewoman to have to work for a living, but all her friends did. The other reason it was kept a secret was because of the type of sewing they did. They made ladies' undergarments—lace camisoles, pantaloons and corsets. Aunt Philadelphia delivered them in neat brown paper parcels to Mr Appleby, the clothier in Sturt Street.

Some of the garments were sent to the city to be sold. Matilda was very proud of this. She wanted to tell people that rich ladies in Melbourne bought her sewing, but she couldn't. Some evenings, Betsy joined the sewing circle to do the mending. Betsy had been threatened with instant dismissal if she told a single soul their secret.

"I won't be sewing this evening, Matilda," Aunt Philadelphia announced. "Mr Chow Mong advised that I rest my arm for a week."

Matilda was delighted at the thought of a night or two off from sewing.

"But you can sew without me."

Matilda sighed and picked up her needle and thread and the camisole she'd been working on. Betsy had finally come back inside and was mending Matilda's school stockings.

"I think my arm is improving, already," said Aunt Philadelphia, rolling up her sleeve.

She inspected the circular marks on her arms.

"Lord above us," Betsy said staring at the purple blotch which was turning yellow around the edges. "What have you let that man do to you?"

"I have great faith in Mr Chow Mong's treatment, Betsy. He is a knowledgeable man."

Betsy grunted.

"I believe he could've become a Mandarin in his own country. He passed the government exams, so I have heard."

"I thought a mandarin was one of those flat oranges with peel that comes off easily," sneered Betsy.

"It is an important Chinese official."

Matilda pricked her finger for the third time and wished that she didn't have to sew every evening. "So why did he come here to be a greengrocer?" she asked.

"I believe the government wanted to arrest him," Aunt Philadelphia said, massaging her arm. "Because he had business with the British."

CHAPTER THREE

Only Birds Can Fly

"TEMPO, MATILDA DEAR," said Mrs Sutton. "This is a folk dance, not a funeral march."

Matilda didn't like the piece. If she'd played it once, she'd played it fifty times. Aunt Philadelphia wanted Matilda to be as accomplished as any young woman in England. She had learned to read at school, of course. She was top of her sewing class because of all the extra practice she got. She'd knitted so many stockings for poor children and soldiers that she was an expert. A gentlewoman needed a musical accomplishment, though. Matilda had to be able to play an instrument as well.

"Limp wrists, my dear," said Mrs Sutton.

Aunt Philadelphia almost had her own piano once. It was a fine piece, inherited from her grandmother. Unfortunately, when it was sent out from England, the ship sank in the middle of the Indian Ocean. So, Aunt Philadelphia had arranged for Matilda to have lessons at Sutton's House of Music in Bridge Street opposite the greengrocery. Mrs Sutton gave her lessons every Saturday morning.

"That's better. Now, let's practise our arpeggios, shall we?"

Matilda enjoyed playing the piano, but she was bored with the lessons. She had been learning for five years now and she played very well. She could play most of the sheet music on the shelves of Sutton's House of Music. But, Mrs Sutton didn't want to stop teaching her. For the past two years, instead of paying for her lessons, Matilda had been playing the pianos out in the showroom to entertain the customers. Mr and Mrs Sutton liked this arrangement, as piano sales had doubled.

Matilda checked her watch. "It's eleven o'clock, Mrs Sutton. I should be out in the showroom."

"So it is. Off you go, dear."

The showroom was full of every musical instrument imaginable, from oboes to penny whistles, from violins to ukeleles. There were seven pianos. A new one had just arrived from Germany. It was a beautiful instrument, a black, shiny grand piano. Matilda sat on the padded stool, chose a piece of music, arranged her skirts and began to play. She loved playing the pianos in Sutton's House of Music. Sometimes, she imagined she was a famous pianist playing in a concert hall. Sometimes, she just closed her eyes and felt the notes vibrating up her arms and inside her chest.

Mr Sutton was a very musical man who could turn his hand to any instrument without instruction. When the Suttons had arrived in the colonies, they lived in a tent on the gold fields. Mr Sutton had made himself a concertina to pass the time in the evenings. Everyone around him loved the music and always pressed him to play a tune. So, Mr Sutton had given up digging for gold and opened the House of Music to bring musical instruments to Ballarat. Mrs Sutton had told Matilda the story at least fifty times. That first concertina was in a glass case in the showroom.

Matilda played the expensive pianos. They sounded beautiful and that's what Mr Sutton liked. Within a few minutes, Matilda's music had attracted a crowd of customers. Outside, more people listened from the footpath. Plenty of customers bought the cheaper pianos that sounded thin and tinny, but they all hoped they'd sound like Matilda on the new German piano. She played for an hour and would have played longer if she hadn't been interrupted.

"I've got something to show you, Matilda." It was a pale, thin boy wearing dark-rimmed glasses.

Matilda looked at the strange contraption he was carrying—a collection of bits of tin, string and off-cuts of wood.

"What is it, Henry?"

Henry was the Suttons' eldest son. He was fourteen, two years older than Matilda. Henry was very clever. The Misses Beasley had taught him everything they could by the time he was nine. He had got bored with school and become his own teacher when he was eleven. He'd read every book in the Public Library.

Henry was like his father in that he could make things from nothing. But Henry built machines and, unfortunately, he didn't have any musical talent at all. He played piano so badly that his father had stopped giving him lessons. He couldn't sing in tune, either. Henry was a big disappointment to his father.

"It's an ornithopter."

Matilda got up from the piano and ran her hand over the smooth wood of the lid, wishing that she could have such a piano at home.

"What does it do?" she asked.

"You'll see."

Henry led Matilda through the back streets to an abandoned gold mine on the edge of town.

He put down his machine. It had two long pieces of tin attached to the top like wings. Henry turned a metal key. The machine started to make a whirring noise. Henry moved a lever and stood back. The two pieces of tin started to flap, getting faster and faster. The whirring became louder, more high-pitched, almost musical.

"It's working!" Henry shouted over the growing noise. He always went red in the face when he was excited.

The machine lifted off the ground ever so slightly. The noise changed to a jarring, clanging noise like nails rattling in a tin. The machine tilted and landed on its side so that one of the flapping pieces of tin dug into the earth and broke off. Henry didn't look at all disappointed.

"Did you see that?" he asked excitedly. "It took off!"

"It barely lifted off the ground," said Matilda, laughing. "What was it meant to do?"

"Fly!"

Matilda looked at the crumpled pieces of tin on the ground and then up at a sulphur-crested cockatoo flying above their heads.

"Birds fly, Henry. They have wings and feathers. But, you can't make bits of tin and wood fly."

Henry smiled knowingly. Matilda was always making fun of his inventions, but he never minded.

"I'd better go home," Matilda said. "I'll be late for dinner."

Matilda went home by the back lanes so that she could run without anyone seeing her. She needn't have bothered hurrying. When she got home, dinner was ready, but Aunt Philadelphia wasn't there. Betsy was annoyed.

"Someone's decided to turn up at last!" she said, banging pots about on the range. "Twenty past one and not a sign of your aunt."

Matilda was surprised. Usually, her aunt was very punctual.

"Where is she? That's what I'd like to know," continued Betsy. "Out she goes in her best hat this morning without a word to me."

The clock chimed the half-hour. Matilda had never known her aunt to be late for dinner before. On Saturday afternoons, after dinner, they always went for a walk. If there was time, they went as far as the Botanical Gardens.

This was Matilda's second favourite thing in the world, after playing the pianos at Suttons. At this rate, there wouldn't be time to go all the way to the Botanical Gardens, they would have to make do with a walk in the eucalypt plantation down the middle of Sturt Street.

Matilda knew there was something wrong as soon as Aunt Philadelphia walked in. For a start, she didn't tell Matilda off for sitting in front of the range like a scullery maid with her shoes off warming her feet. Then she left her hat on the kitchen table instead of putting it in its box. By this time, Betsy was fuming.

"There's five shillings worth of good mutton overcooked in the oven," she said.

"I'm sure an extra half-hour has not made it inedible, Betsy," replied Aunt Philadelphia calmly. "Here is something for dessert."

Betsy folded her arms and refused to take the parcel Aunt Philadelphia was holding out. Matilda opened it.

"Strawberries!" she said. "I've never seen strawberries of such a size and colour."

"Where did you get them?" asked Betsy. "Don't tell me you've walked all the way to the greengrocer's for a basket of strawberries."

Aunt Philadelphia didn't reply. She wiggled her fingers. In the two months since her first treatment, Mr Chow Mong had completely cured the pains in her arm.

They sat down to dinner. Betsy slapped the potatoes and mutton onto their plates and then sat down at the table to eat with them. Servants were supposed to eat in the kitchen, but Betsy had eaten her dinner in the dining room since Matilda was a child and had needed someone to feed her.

Aunt Philadelphia had bright pink spots on her cheeks and her forehead glistened slightly.

"Are you ill, Aunt?" Matilda asked with a little tremble in her voice. Elizabeth Wyatt's mother had recently died of consumption, just like her own mother.

"No, I'm not ill, but I do have something to tell you. Something that will affect us all." Aunt Philadelphia smoothed her black skirts carefully, then she took a deep breath. "I am to be married."

Matilda and Betsy both stared at Aunt Philadelphia and then at each other.

"The wedding will take place at the end of next month."

Betsy's mouth was hanging open like an empty coalscuttle. Matilda opened her mouth but couldn't get out any words. Who on earth could Aunt Philadelphia be marrying? She was old, almost thirty-five, so the two eligible young men they knew were out of the question. The only widower of their acquaintance had fallen down dead by the side of the road just the week before.

"Who are you to marry?" asked Matilda.

"Mr Chow Mong," Aunt Philadelphia replied with a smile.

"The greengrocer!" exclaimed Matilda.

"Lord above us," said Betsy. "She's taken leave of her senses."

"But you can't marry him, Aunt. He's Chinese!" Matilda tried to talk her aunt out of her absurd plan. "I know Mr Chow Mong's treatment has cured the pains in your arm, Aunt," she said, "but surely that doesn't mean you have to marry him."

Aunt Philadelphia refused to discuss the subject. All she would say was that God had given her a sign.

The news was all over town by dinner time the next day. Women from the Temperance Society called in and tried to bring Aunt Philadelphia to her senses. She listened, then politely told them that her senses were intact.

"It's the herbs," Betsy said the following evening. "That man's mixed some sort of evil potion to make you marry him so that he can bring you to ruin."

Aunt Philadelphia sighed over her needlework. "The treatment cured the pains in my arm, Betsy, but had no effect on my mind."

"So why has a sensible, God-fearing woman like you got it into her head to marry a Chinaman? That's what I want to know."

Nothing would persuade Aunt Philadelphia to change her mind, not a visit from Reverend Binks nor a group of women from the Wesleyan Ladies Committee who stood outside the front door for hours at a time saying prayers. At first Reverend Binks refused to have anything to do with the ceremony, but when Aunt Philadelphia threatened to marry at another church, he agreed. The wedding took place at the end of the month at the Wesleyan Manse where the minister lived. Matilda, Betsy and the minister's wife were the only ones at the ceremony.

CHAPTER FOUR
Mixed Blessings

MATILDA LOOKED across the dining table. Mr Chow Mong was carefully cutting a piece of cold meat as if he wasn't quite familiar with the use of a knife and fork. Once the meat was cut up, getting a piece to stay on his fork was more than he could manage. He lay down his knife and fork as if he'd had enough to eat. He sipped his tea from one of the best china cups instead. He could manage that quite well.

Aunt Philadelphia had done her best to transform Mr Chow Mong into a gentleman. He now wore a suit with a waistcoat and a fob watch. His pigtail had been cut off, his moustache trimmed and he had a proper haircut, which Aunt Philadelphia had styled herself with her sewing scissors. She had also given him the name William. Matilda was supposed to call him Uncle William. None of this made any difference, though. He was still Chinese. Aunt Philadelphia smiled at him from her side of the table. Betsy now ate all her meals in the kitchen. Matilda wished she was out there in the kitchen with her. She also wished she didn't have to go back to school.

Matilda had had two days off school to help her aunt rearrange the house. A new double bed had been purchased for Aunt Philadelphia's bedroom. A new armchair for Uncle William's use appeared in the parlour.

Aunt Philadelphia had supervised the purchase of an entire wardrobe of clothing for her husband. She had also bought new curtains for the dining room and these had to be hemmed and hung. Aunt Philadelphia had forbidden anything Chinese in the house. Uncle William's things arrived in a small, carved camphorwood box, which remained closed.

Matilda thought it was strange how a bed, one chair and a pair of curtains had made the house seem like a completely different place.

Now she had to face her school friends. After a mouthful of toast and a sip of tea, she excused herself from the breakfast table. Aunt Philadelphia followed Matilda into her room.

"You must tell your teacher that you have changed your name, Matilda."

"Changed my name?"

"Since your Uncle William has accepted responsibility for your upbringing, I think it's only fair that you take his name, as I have."

It was true, Aunt Philadelphia had sent out cards advising her acquaintances to address correspondence to Mrs William Chow Mong.

"I won't take such an outlandish name."

"Matilda, your uncle could have sent you off to the orphanage."

"I don't care. I'm keeping my father's name!"

"Matilda, what's wrong with you?"

Matilda had never defied her aunt before.

"You can't make me change my name. I won't!"

At school, it was as bad as Matilda had expected. Elizabeth Wyatt made loud comments about there being a strong smell of cabbage and onion in the classroom when Matilda entered.

Victoria Brittingham came over and peered at her face. "Aren't you feeling well, Matilda?" she asked with mock concern. "Your face has a yellowish look to it."

All the girls giggled. Matilda didn't speak.

Sophie Stevenson, who had been Matilda's best friend since they started school, was sitting between Elizabeth and Victoria. Normally, she saved a place next to her for Matilda. Sophie didn't look at her. Matilda sat by herself at the end of the front row. Since her very first day, Matilda had loved school. She knew from now on she was going to hate it.

When she went home for lunch (they had dinner in the evenings now when Uncle William got home) Matilda was glad to find that Aunt Philadelphia was out with the Wesleyan Ladies Committee. That meant that she could eat in the kitchen with Betsy.

"No-one will talk to me at school," Matilda said, taking a big bite out of her bread and dripping. Aunt Philadelphia had forbidden Matilda to eat such common food. "And I don't really blame them."

"It's just not right. A Christian woman

marrying a Chinese man," Betsy said. "She'll come to her senses one day and then she'll be sorry for what she's done."

The afternoon at school was the same. No-one wanted to be Matilda's dancing partner, she wasn't given a part in the school theatrical performance and Sophie walked home with Elizabeth and Victoria. Matilda didn't feel like going straight home. Instead, she walked to Sutton's House of Music. Henry was working on the accounts. He was no good at selling instruments in the showroom (he wanted to explain to the customers the laws of physics that made each instrument work), but his father hoped that his mathematical abilities might be of use to the family business. Henry had the accounts ledger open, but he wasn't paying any attention to it. He was drawing a complicated diagram on a piece of paper.

"I know exactly where I went wrong with the ornithopter," he said as Matilda flopped down in a chair.

"My friends won't speak to me," said Matilda.

"It's all to do with the angle of the blades."

"You're not listening to me, Henry."

"Why aren't your friends speaking to you?"

"Because my aunt has gone mad and got married to that man, of course."

"I didn't know your aunt had married," replied Henry, putting down his pen. "Who did she marry?"

"Henry!" cried Matilda in exasperation. "You must be the only person in Ballarat who hasn't heard. She married Mr Chow Mong, the greengrocer."

"That's no reason for your friends to stop speaking to you."

"They think it is."

"Mr Chow Mong is a nice man. His shop is across the street. He used to give me fruit when I was younger. I like him."

"It's easy for you to say that. You don't have a foreigner who hardly knows how to use a knife and fork sitting opposite you at the breakfast table."

Matilda folded her arms. There was no-one who understood what she was going through.

Though you would never have known it from his two rooms behind the greengrocery, Uncle William was well-off. His income meant that Aunt Philadelphia didn't have to do the sewing, any more. It also meant that a girl could be employed to help Betsy with the laundry and accompany Aunt Philadelphia to order the food on Wednesdays. Matilda could go to school on Monday mornings.

In the evenings, Matilda, her aunt and her new uncle all sat in the parlour. There was no sewing to do, so Matilda was free to play the piano that Uncle William had purchased from Sutton's House of Music. It was a good quality English upright that had a fine tone and brass candle holders. But it didn't give her as much pleasure as she'd imagined when she'd dreamed of having her own piano.

Aunt Philadelphia's main task was to make Uncle William into a good Christian. She read passages from the Bible to him every night. Matilda had to read to her uncle as well. Her job was to read the newspapers so that he was up with current events. The *Star* and the *Evening Post* were delivered daily.

Every Saturday, the three of them walked in the Botanical Gardens. Matilda didn't enjoy it. Everyone stared at them. Children pointed at Uncle William. Matilda knew that the boys who were laughing at them would have thrown stones at Uncle William if he'd been alone. Aunt Philadelphia didn't seem to notice them. She strolled around on her husband's arm, teaching him the English names of plants. Uncle William smiled at his wife. Matilda often wondered why he had married her strict aunt—and why she had married him. The only conclusion she had come to was that they liked each other's company.

CHAPTER FIVE

Shades of Pink

Miss Ann Beasley hung a map of the world on the blackboard. She pointed out all the areas that were coloured pink. These were the countries that belonged to the British Empire. There were splotches of pink all over the map.

"We should be very proud to be part of such a great Empire, girls," Miss Beasley said. "With God on our side, we British will soon be rulers of the world."

She showed them the newest colony, Basutoland, a little country in southern Africa.

"There isn't another country in the world with so many colonies." Miss Beasley pointed to China on the map. "Take China, for instance.

A large country, an enormous population, but not a single colony. This is the sign of a weak nation populated by inferior people."

Matilda could see all the girls turning to sneak a look at her, as if she was personally responsible for the Chinese nation. School no longer gave her any pleasure. She wished she didn't have to go.

After school she went home and could hear Betsy laughing in the kitchen with Lizzie, the new day-maid. Lizzie was a silly girl with red hair, not much older than Matilda, and she was sitting in the chair where Matilda always used to sit. She couldn't even sit and have a cup of tea and a biscuit with Betsy any more.

Matilda waited a few weeks for things to settle down and get back to normal. She didn't play with friends from school any more, so most days, she visited Henry at the House of Music.

"We learned about China today," she told Henry. "Miss Beasley says it's a weak nation and that the Chinese are inferior to Europeans, only capable of doing work that doesn't need much thought. She says they're good at imitating what they see other people do, but they don't have the type of brain to be able to create anything themselves."

Henry laughed loudly.

"It's not funny, Henry," Matilda said.

"It's extremely funny. Ridiculous, even. The Chinese have invented any number of things." He counted them off on his fingers.

"The clock, the compass, gunpowder, paddle-wheel boats, the stirrup." He thought a bit more. "Paper, printing. The Chinese were printing books a thousand years before people in England. They built the Great Wall of China in 300 BC. It's 2000 kilometres long. Can you imagine it? Do you know what the British were constructing then?"

Matilda didn't know.

"Earth mounds," Henry told her.

Unlike Miss Ann Beasley, the Reverend Binks, the ladies from the Temperance Society, Betsy and every other person in Ballarat (apart from Henry), Aunt Philadelphia did not believe that the Chinese were an inferior race. She believed that all of the heathen peoples of the world had wandered from God's path. This had happened shortly after Noah's flood. They had forgotten about God. All they had to do was become Christians and they would be equal to everyone else.

Matilda waited a few more weeks, three months in fact, for things to be normal. They didn't. She knew then that things were never going to be the same again. She had to start being more careful about what she wished for. Her wishes had a nasty habit of coming true, but things never turned out as she imagined. Having all the things she'd wanted so badly hadn't made her life better. It had made it worse. She would have given anything to have her old life back again—the smell of hot soapy water in the early morning, the blister on her thumb from sewing, a pianoless parlour.

Matilda thought she must have done something terribly wrong to make her life take such a horrible turn. She resolved to be very good. She would join the hymn singers outside public houses on Saturday nights. She would visit the old people in the benevolent asylum every week. She would knit more stockings for poor people. At least she had the comfort that things couldn't get any worse. Or so she thought.

One Thursday, Matilda arrived home from school to find the doctor's carriage outside the gate. She rushed inside. Aunt Philadelphia's bedroom door was closed. Betsy was sitting in the kitchen with her head in her apron. Lizzie was as white as a bleached sheet.

"What's happened, Betsy?" asked Matilda. "What's wrong with Aunt Philadelphia?"

"She was walking to the Temperance Society luncheon," replied Betsy. "And she fainted away in the middle of Sturt Street. Two cabbies had to carry her to the footpath."

"What's wrong with her?"

"I don't know. The doctor's been in there for three-quarters of an hour. It's all that visiting the sick. She's caught some disease."

"More likely it's something she caught running around after that Chinaman," said Lizzie. "Everybody says she was mad to marry him."

Fortunately, Dr Berger came into the kitchen before they could think of worse things that may have happened to Aunt Philadelphia.

"Is it bad, Doctor?" asked Betsy, twisting her apron into a rope.

"Not at all," said the doctor with a smile. "Good news, in fact." He turned to Matilda. "You are to have a baby brother or sister."

Betsy cried out and collapsed on a chair. Lizzie started to sob. Matilda didn't say a word, not even to correct the doctor and tell him it would be a cousin.

The doctor continued to smile. "Mrs Chow Mong is rather old to be having a first child, so we must take great care of her," he said. "No more walking into town. The Temperance Society must manage without her. She mustn't wear any tight clothing. Definitely no stays."

The colour suddenly came back to Lizzie's

cheeks at the mention of female undergarments.

"She must rest with her feet up as much as possible. As far as I can tell, the baby is due in about five months."

When Uncle William came home that evening, he found the house in chaos. There was no dinner for him. Betsy had been too busy making beef tea, lemon and barley water, and calf's-foot broth for the invalid. When Aunt Philadelphia told him the news, Uncle William smiled broadly.

Mrs Perkins, the president of the Wesleyan Ladies Committee, visited Aunt Philadelphia the following afternoon. Aunt Philadelphia was by this time convalescing in the parlour.

"We'll pray for you," said Mrs Perkins. "God has His reasons for sending us trials."

Aunt Philadelphia actually seemed quite pleased about the coming event.

"Other women have managed to survive motherhood," she said sipping her beef tea.

"How fortunate that you have Matilda to help you through this difficulty," said Mrs Perkins. "She'll be leaving school, of course."

"That won't be necessary, Eloise."

"She can read and write and sew. What more does a girl need to know?" continued Mrs Perkins. "It's common knowledge that too much schooling for girls isn't healthy."

The size of Aunt Philadelphia's stomach grew at an alarming rate. After another month, she was far too large to be seen in public. Matilda had to make the weekly visits to the butcher, the baker and the dairy. She memorised her aunt's instructions about the length of sausages, the colour of the crust on the bread and the maturity of cheese.

Aunt Philadelphia became tired more often, so someone had to read to her. Naturally, the job fell to Matilda who now went to school less and less.

The date that the doctor had predicted for the birth came and went. Aunt Philadelphia was now permanently in bed. The slightest exercise exhausted her. The doctor visited daily. He frowned. Uncle William stopped smiling. Dr Berger decided the birth was not going to happen naturally. He would have to surgically remove the baby. This was enough for Aunt Philadelphia's birth pangs to start.

SHADES OF PINK   49

It was a long birth. A night and another day passed. Matilda and Uncle William spent much time together in the parlour in total silence listening to the awful sounds of Aunt Philadelphia's pain. Finally, at five past midnight on the second day, a baby girl was born. That wasn't the end of it though. The reason for all the problems was now made clear. Another baby was born. Twin girls. If Matilda had had any idea that things would settle down after the birth, she was very, very wrong.

Chapter Six

Too Many Women

THE BABIES WERE called Margaret May and Hannah Lily. Matilda would never have thought that two tiny babies could cause such chaos. Aunt Philadelphia was well enough to get out of bed in a month, but her whole day was filled with feeding the two babies and resting to be ready for the next feed. It seemed that one of them was always awake and needing attention. Aunt Philadelphia rarely managed to be out of her nightgown by lunch time and her hair stayed in an untidy plait all day. She always had a slightly confused look on her face, as if she was trying to work out the answer to a puzzle. Dozens of napkins, nightdresses, vests and cot sheets were added to the piles of things that had to be washed. Betsy needed both Matilda and Lizzie to help her on wash days.

Matilda soon gave up school entirely. She took her turn to walk a grizzly baby around the nursery at any hour of the day or night. The babies were gradually introduced to the open air and taken for walks in perambulators. This was one chore Matilda didn't mind. She would walk to the Botanical Gardens if she had her way, but Lizzie thought it was too far.

Walking was the one thing that always kept the babies happy. They never cried when they were being walked in their prams, no matter how bumpy the footpath. The only problem was that every other person stopped them to look at the girls. It seemed that the whole of Ballarat knew about the half-Chinese twins and wanted to get a look at them.

"The poor little things," Lizzie said every time someone peered into the prams. "What will become of them when they grow up? No-one will want to marry them."

Matilda looked at her little cousins. They each had black hair that refused to sit neatly under a knitted bonnet and poked out in all directions. They had brown eyes, sweet little mouths, and chubby brown hands which waved about above their blankets.

Just as things started to settle into a routine, the babies got sick. Margaret developed colic and Hannah contracted whooping cough. Betsy now spent all of her time as nurse to Aunt Philadelphia and the babies. Lizzie worked every day and moved into the house. Everyone got even less sleep and Aunt Philadelphia started to look ill herself.

Sometimes, Matilda found it difficult to imagine that this pale, frail woman was the same aunt who used to walk so fast that Matilda couldn't keep up with her. Indeed, the same woman who had bashed a drunken miner over the head with her "Drink is the Instrument of the Devil" placard.

One Saturday, Uncle William called Matilda into the parlour where he was sitting at the writing desk. He was finishing a letter. The letter was written in Chinese and he wrote with a fine brush not a pen. He blotted the letter, folded it and put it in an envelope. On the envelope, he wrote some more Chinese characters. Only at the bottom did he write a single English word—China.

"I would like you to take this letter to the post office yourself please, Ma-til-da."

He had a strange way of saying English names with equal emphasis on each of the sounds. He could barely manage all the syllables in his wife's name and usually called her "my dear", or when speaking to Matilda and Betsy, "your aunt" or "your mistress".

"I do not trust Li-zzie," he said.

Lizzie was frightened of Uncle William, who had a habit of staring at her red hair. In fact, she was frightened of anything Chinese. She was likely to take one look at the Chinese writing and throw the letter in the bushes.

Matilda was always glad to get out of the house. As she walked to the post office, she thought about Uncle William. She'd never considered that he had relatives still in China. She handed the letter over to the post mistress who looked at the strange writing and then at Matilda with suspicion. Matilda watched the letter as it was stamped and thrown into a box. She hadn't even been as far as Melbourne or seen the ocean. She had never been further than Sandhurst. That little letter was going to sail all the way to China.

As soon as it was posted, Matilda forgot all about the letter and was drawn back into the world that revolved around Margaret and Hannah. Hannah got over her whooping cough, and everyone became used to walking Margaret around the house between five and seven in the evening while she screamed with colic. So, it was with great surprise that

Matilda opened the front door one morning and found the same letter on the front door step. It was creased, grubby with much handling and clutched in the hand of a small Chinese woman who was standing next to two large Chinese boxes. She was leaning on a walking stick with a lion's head handle.

The Chinese woman was complaining loudly about something, possibly lots of things, but no-one could understand her. Uncle William had left for work. Betsy and Aunt Philadelphia came and stared at the woman on the doorstep. Lizzie hid in the pantry.

The woman sat down on her box. Matilda noticed that she had tiny little feet.

"We should invite her in," said Matilda.

"We'll do no such thing," replied Aunt Philadelphia. "We have no idea who she is."

"She must be a relative of Uncle William's. I posted that letter for him months ago."

Aunt Philadelphia looked at the woman wearing black pyjamas and a bamboo hat and decided she needed a lie-down. Matilda sent Lizzie to get Uncle William.

As soon as Uncle William walked in the gate, the woman started talking in Chinese.

"This is my mother," explained Uncle William when she finally paused.

Matilda went to get Aunt Philadelphia and to tell Lizzie to come out of the pantry and put the kettle on. Everyone sat at the kitchen table. Uncle William pointed to them, explaining who they were. He left Aunt Philadelphia till last. The two women glared at each other.

As if she knew she was being left out of something, Margaret started crying. Hannah soon joined in.

"Lizzie, help me fetch the babies," Matilda said, thinking they might break the ice between

Aunt Philadelphia and her strange mother-in-law. "Betsy, the kettle will boil dry if someone doesn't make the tea soon."

The babies were now six months old. Hannah smiled at the familiar faces, but her smile faded when she saw the strange woman in black. Her lip quivered and she started to cry. Margaret joined in immediately. The Chinese woman looked at the babies, but not with pleasure. She looked around the table at them all and back to Uncle William.

"*Taai do neui-yan*," she said.

They all turned to Uncle William. He looked uncomfortable.

"What did she say?" asked Matilda.

"Too many women," he replied.

"What should we call her?" Matilda asked.

"Po Po. It means Granny."

"And where will she stay?"

"It will have to be your room, Ma-til-da."

Aunt Philadelphia said nothing. She sat at the kitchen table with Margaret on her lap. Uncle William helped haul the boxes to Matilda's room, then went back to the shop.

When Po Po opened one of her Chinese boxes, a strange foreign smell filled the room.

She began to take things out—cooking pots, strange foods, vases, painted scrolls.

Aunt Philadelphia suddenly strode into the room. "I will have no Chinese things in my house," she said slamming the box shut. Po Po didn't need a translator to understand.

That night, Matilda lay on a mattress on the floor unable to sleep. Matilda had always had a room of her own. She was used to peace and privacy. Po Po snored. Whenever Matilda drifted off to sleep, she was suddenly jarred awake again by the snoring.

The next morning, Po Po was up early. As soon as she had her room to herself, Matilda fell asleep immediately. But she was woken soon after by a strange smell coming from the kitchen. She got up and put on her dressing gown. Po Po was cooking in her deep, round-bottomed frying pan. Matilda had no idea what was in it. The kettle was boiling. Po Po poured the boiling water into a big tin mug with flowers stencilled on the side. She took a pinch of tea-leaves from a tin and threw them into the mug. She covered the mug with a lid.

Po Po ignored Matilda. She scooped whatever was in the pan into a bowl decorated with dragons. She was just about to lift some of the mysterious breakfast to her mouth with a pair of black lacquered chopsticks, when Aunt Philadelphia burst into the kitchen. She was fully dressed and her hair was tied up in a bun.

"There will be no Chinese things in my house," she said picking up the bowl with the dragons on it, the lidded mug and the tin of tea. She took them to the backdoor and hurled them out into the garden.

Aunt Philadelphia then marched into Matilda's room and came out again with an armful of things. Po Po was shouting in Chinese, trying to take back her belongings.

All the strength that Aunt Philadelphia had been lacking over the past year suddenly flowed back into her. Betsy added to the uproar by shouting "Lord above us" regularly. The babies were howling in the nursery. Lizzie came in the back gate with the milk and was greeted with a shower of cooking spoons and chopsticks.

"Aunt," shouted Matilda, taking a lovely vase from her just as she was about to launch it at the back fence. "You'll injure yourself. Let me take the things outside, there's no need to ruin the parsley patch."

Aunt Philadelphia stopped, chest heaving.

"Betsy, Lizzie," said Matilda. "Take care of the babies. Aunt, perhaps you should rest."

Aunt Philadelphia brushed back the hair that was beginning to escape from her bun and did as she was told. Matilda was left in the garden with Po Po among the litter of Chinese goods. She began to pick up the things. The dragon bowl was broken, the lidded mug was dented, the tea tin was empty.

Chapter Seven
A Little Piece of China

It was the strangest Sunday Matilda had ever known. No-one went to church. Matilda couldn't remember Aunt Philadelphia ever missing church. She gave Betsy and Lizzie the the whole day off. She locked herself in her room all day with the babies. Uncle William sat in his parlour chair staring at the empty fire grate. Matilda read all day. Po Po spent the day in the garden, sitting in the sun like a cat.

When Betsy and Lizzie returned, they showed no signs of making supper. Matilda began to realise that the household would grind to a halt if she didn't do something.

"Betsy, we will all collapse from hunger soon if we don't have something to eat," she said.

"It's too late to start cooking now, and the fire in the range is almost out."

"Well, you better get it going again. We've got leftover chicken, haven't we? Fry it up with some shallots, boil some potatoes and…make a salad. Then we can have the quince preserve with custard. Lizzie, put on some water for the babies' bath."

Matilda knocked on her Aunt's door.

"Aunt Philadelphia, it's time to bathe Margaret and Hannah."

To Matilda's surprise, her aunt opened the door.

Within half-an-hour, there was a fire in the parlour, the babies were happily splashing in their bathwater and the smell of cooking chicken was coming from the kitchen. Now there was just the problem of the large black boxes that were still in Matilda's room.

"Perhaps we could store your mother's things in the stable," she suggested to Uncle William. "Until something else is arranged."

He seemed relieved that someone had

found something for him to do and jumped to his feet. They didn't own a horse, so the stable was used as a storage room. Uncle William carried the boxes into the stable. Po Po followed with her dented mug and empty tea tin.

Supper was a very quiet affair. Matilda and Uncle William ate their potatoes and fried chicken hungrily. Aunt Philadelphia nibbled at her salad. Po Po picked up her knife and fork and then put them down again. She didn't know how to get the food to her mouth. Po Po sadly watched Betsy clear away her untouched plate. She knew how to handle a spoon though and ate two helpings of quince and custard.

That night Matilda lay awake again. The sounds of Po Po's rumbling stomach added to the muttered complaints in Chinese when she was awake and the snoring when she was asleep. What could possibly be done? Aunt Philadelphia wouldn't be able to transform Po Po into an acceptable gentlewoman the way she'd transformed Uncle William into a gentleman. They could hardly turn Uncle William's mother out onto the street. Matilda was careful not to wish for anything. She'd had enough changes to last her a lifetime.

The next morning, Po Po had solved the problem herself. Matilda found her arranging her things around the stable. She moved slowly and awkwardly on her tiny feet, which were only a few centimetres long. With Matilda's help, she dragged the old mattress from the bedroom into the stable.

Aunt Philadelphia and Po Po never tried to communicate with each other. Lizzie refused to go out into the garden by herself. (She said she'd seen Po Po kill chickens by looking at them.) Within a fortnight, everyone had accepted that there was a Chinese woman living in the stable and cooking strange food on a fire in the garden.

Margaret and Hannah were weaned and Aunt Philadelphia started to take up her charity work again. Now that the babies were older, Matilda was no longer needed every minute of the day. The washing still took up Mondays from morning till night and she walked the babies every afternoon with Lizzie, but there was no sewing to do any more and Lizzie did all Matilda's old chores.

Matilda sat in the kitchen. She wasn't used

to idleness. She could see Po Po sleeping in a cane chair outside in the sun. The old woman intrigued her. What did she do all day in the stable?

She went out into the garden and opened the stable door slowly. It was dark inside. There was only one small window, which was covered with a curtain. Matilda went in. There was a strong smell, sweet but sickly. The wedge of light from the doorway illuminated a carpet on the earth floor. On the walls hung scrolls, some covered with Chinese writing, some with paintings of mountains and flowers.

As Matilda's eyes grew used to the dim light, she could make out more things—a low table, shiny black with pieces of mother-of-pearl set into it, a tiny little teapot that would have fitted into her hand, and a huge vase full of peacock feathers.

The thing that caught her eye most of all was a cabinet carved with delicate flowers and birds. It had little doors and drawers with brass handles. A tiny curved bridge led from one shelf to another. Matilda couldn't imagine how all these things had fitted into the boxes Po Po had brought from China.

66 CARELESS WISHES

The sweet, sickly smell was even stronger over that side of the room. There was also a faint glow. Matilda looked closer. The light was coming from a small oil lamp. Thin wisps of smoke spiralled up from burning sticks. The lamp and the burning sticks were in front of a picture of a Chinese man dressed in coloured robes with a long black beard and a fierce expression on his bright red face. Arranged around the picture were an orange, a bun and something else. Matilda looked closer. She saw feathers and claws—and two dead eyes staring at her. It was a dead chicken. She turned and ran out of the stable—straight into Po Po.

A Little Piece of China   67

Matilda expected the woman to be angry. She didn't shout at her though, she spoke to Matilda in a pleading voice as if she wanted her to do something. Unfortunately, Matilda couldn't understand a word.

Matilda felt sorry for the old woman. How lonely she must feel in a foreign country, unable to go anywhere and only able to speak to Uncle William. Matilda made some tea and took it into the garden on a tray. The old woman stopped grumbling to herself. They both sat in silence and drank their tea. There were a lot of questions that Matilda would have liked to ask. There were things she wanted to know, such as why there was a dead chicken in the stable, but the two of them sat and said nothing. Matilda had an idea though.

"Henry, I want to go to the Chinese village," Matilda said.

Henry was building a new ornithopter.

"You have to come with me," she explained. "I can't go there on my own."

"Why do you want to go there at all?"

"I need to find an interpreter so that I can understand what Po Po wants."

"Can't you ask your uncle?"

"No, I cannot."

Henry had learned not to argue with Matilda.

The narrow main street in the Chinese village looked very different to the main streets in Ballarat. The buildings were rough wooden huts. Nothing looked like it was built to last. The signs above the shops were all in Chinese and the street was crowded with Chinese people. They were all black-clad Chinese men, most with pigtails and broad cane sunhats. There were no Europeans and not a single woman or child. Every man stared at Henry and Matilda. They were the foreigners, here.

Matilda's plan suddenly seemed very silly. There were lots of people who spoke Chinese, but did any of them speak English? She was just about to tell Henry she had changed her mind when she saw a face she recognised. There in an eating-house at the table near the door was Uncle William eating rice and vegetables with chopsticks.

"Matilda! What are you doing here?" Uncle William asked looking very guilty.

"I was about to ask you the same thing." Matilda looked around the dim room. It had an earth floor, three rough tables and benches. It didn't look at all like a respectable place to be eating in.

"You better sit down," Uncle William said.

Someone brought a pot of tea and three little teacups without handles. Uncle William hadn't finished his lunch. The waiter brought a stack of bamboo baskets. Inside each basket were steaming round buns.

"Would you like something to eat? The dumplings are very good."

Henry said he hadn't had lunch and would be delighted to join him. Next came bowls full of long thin strings with pieces of vegetables and meat mixed in.

"Noodles," Uncle William told them.

Henry picked up his chopsticks, muttered something about levers and fulcrums and soon managed to pick up one of the dumplings. Matilda stared at the chopsticks. It seemed impossible that anyone could eat with two wooden sticks. Uncle William called out to the waiter who ran outside and came back several minutes later with a bent and tarnished fork.

Even though she wasn't really hungry, Matilda ate three of the pork-filled dumplings and half a bowl of noodles. The food tasted surprisingly good.

"So," said Uncle William. "What are you doing in Golden Point?"

"Matilda is looking for an interpreter," Henry said.

Matilda kicked him under the table.

"Why do you need an interpreter? I can translate for you," said Uncle William.

"I want to be able to talk to Po Po myself."

"You need to learn Chinese to do that."

A Little Piece of China 71

Matilda listened to the garbled sounds that the Chinese men around them were making. She couldn't imagine them ever making sense.

"If I could just say a few things. Even hello, thank you, yes and no would be a help."

"It's not like learning French, you know," said Uncle William. "Chinese is nothing like European languages."

"I could try. You could teach me."

"Your aunt would not allow it."

"She doesn't have to know," replied Matilda slyly. "The same as she doesn't have to know where you have lunch."

Uncle William put his chopsticks down guiltily and then smiled. "Very well. We will meet here every Thursday."

Uncle William was right. The Chinese language was nothing like French or English. The words were all short and sharp. There were no verb endings to learn, no plurals, no masculine or feminine words. There were tones though. Each little word could be pronounced with eleven different tones, which were high, low or going up or down. It was a bit like singing.

Uncle William was a very good teacher.

He never shouted at her like the Misses Beasley. His lessons never sent her to sleep. His classroom was the Chinese village. Every Thursday, they would walk about the streets and go into different shops. At first, Matilda didn't feel safe, but she soon grew used to the place. As she learned the language, she met all sorts of unusual people: the kitemaker who made butterfly and fish kites; the paper cutter who cut coloured paper into fantastic dragons and princesses; the temple guard who sat next to the lion outside the temple. The Chinese men grew used to seeing Matilda and stopped staring. Some even greeted her and she returned their greeting.

In two months, Matilda learned enough Chinese to buy little things in the shops and to ask directions. She could also order food in the Golden Phoenix eating-house. The first time Matilda spoke to Po Po in Chinese, the old woman dropped her mug in surprise and then invited Matilda into the stable.

It no longer seemed scary inside the stable. The curtain was pulled back, the door was open and sunlight fell on all the strange and beautiful things. Matilda could look at all the scrolls as she sipped her tea, admiring the embroidered fans and the carved detail of the cabinet. Po Po talked non-stop for at least five minutes, ticking off a list of complaints on her fingers. She spoke too fast and Matilda could not understand a word.

Po Po thought that Matilda must be very stupid. There were so many Chinese words that she didn't understand. Matilda made her speak slower and they got on a little better. Po Po complained that Aunt Philadelphia hadn't produced any grandsons. She complained about Australians in general—the ridiculous clothes they wore and the awful food they ate.

"They grow no rice," she said shaking her head. "They just dig holes in the ground. Big Noses are all stupid." Matilda had heard other Chinese refer to Europeans as "Big Noses".

Po Po also complained about her son trying to starve her. He brought her vegetables but no bean curd, no noodles, no dried black mushrooms. Matilda knew these words from her visits to the Golden Phoenix. She explained that she could easily buy these things for her, but she had no money. Po Po smiled and went to the carved cabinet. She opened one of the drawers with a small key. She pulled out some gold Chinese coins and gave three to Matilda.

On her next visit to the Chinese village, when her lesson was over and she had said goodbye to Uncle William, she bought the things that Po Po wanted. The shopkeeper was very polite and bowed to her. From then on, Matilda always brought something back from the Chinese village for the old woman. Whether it was a tin of water chestnuts, a stick of incense or a leaflet for a theatre performance, Po Po was always delighted.

Chapter Eight

Feast for the Ancestors

ONE THURSDAY, Matilda bought a treat for Po Po. It was a fruit something like a strawberry covered in sticky toffee on a stick. Po Po thanked Matilda but didn't smile and chuckle to herself as she usually did when Matilda bought her something.

"What's the matter, Po Po?" Matilda asked.

Po Po told her there was a special day coming up and Uncle William had forbidden her to join in the celebrations. She used words that Matilda didn't know: *gwai* and *chung*. Matilda said she'd try and find out what the words meant.

The next Thursday, Matilda successfully asked the paper cutter for a beautiful pink picture of peonies and chrysanthemums and handed him the correct money. Her Chinese was improving.

She had just finished reciting the Chinese numbers from one to fifty without a mistake, when there was a loud explosion. Matilda nearly jumped out of her skin.

"Don't worry," laughed Uncle William. "It's only fireworks."

Sure enough, there were more explosions and sounds of rockets whizzing. Matilda could see showers of coloured sparks in the darkening afternoon sky. Bells and gongs rang out. Cymbals and strange-sounding trumpets began playing. People wearing bright costumes with painted faces paraded down the street.

"There was a big gold find today," Uncle William explained. "Everyone is celebrating. There will be a theatre performance tonight."

"I wish I could see it," said Matilda.

"It's already late," Uncle William said. "You must go home."

Matilda said goodbye and waved as Uncle William headed back to his shop. Once he was out of sight, Matilda went to find the temple guard. He was leaning on the stone lion that guarded the temple door. She asked him the meaning of the words that Po Po had used.

"*Gwai*," he had said struggling to explain in English. "This mean ghost. *Chung*, this is dead people's place. Dead people in holes in the ground."

Matilda couldn't quite make sense of this information, but next time she saw Henry she asked him. Henry had been reading everything he could about China. Since he had read all the books in the Public Library, he had joined the

Mechanics Institute Library and was reading his way through their collection.

"The Chinese worship their dead ancestors and give them offerings of food," Henry explained. "If they don't, they believe the ancestors will get angry and bring them bad luck. They have a holiday called Feast of the Hungry Ghosts. This is for the lonely ghosts with no families of their own, so they don't get angry and play nasty tricks on people. People build a bonfire in the cemetery, make offerings and have a picnic."

Matilda thought that a cemetery was a strange place to have a picnic. When she asked Po Po about it, the old woman's face lit up. That was what she'd been trying to tell Matilda about. The Feast of the Hungry Ghosts was next week and she wanted to go. She had been burning incense and making offerings to her own ancestors, but she had to keep the Hungry Ghosts happy as well.

Henry had also told Matilda why Po Po had such trouble walking.

"Chinese women have their feet bound to keep them small. It's considered elegant. When they are little girls, their toes are bent under.

Then their feet are bound up with bandages and the toes break. So it's very painful for them to walk."

Matilda was horrified. Because of her deformed little feet, Po Po could only just manage to walk to the back gate with the help of her stick. Walking to the Chinese village was beyond her. Getting as far as the cemetery, was an impossibility.

The only way Po Po could possibly get to the cemetery was by horse cab. Matilda had no experience with cabbies. Aunt Philadelphia never took a cab. She thought that people who took cabs were lazy, and that cabbies were impolite and too fond of drinking and gambling. She would walk from one end of town to the other in the rain rather than take a cab.

The cabbies lounged around the edge of the plantation in the middle of Sturt Street. They were waiting for customers. Some leaned on their two-wheeled carriages, with their shirt sleeves rolled up and their hats pushed back. Others sat on benches, smoking and laughing. Matilda approached them timidly. She had just plucked up the courage to speak when she saw Mrs Perkins, the president of the Wesleyan

Ladies Committee, come striding toward her. Matilda ducked behind a horse.

"You there," said Mrs Perkins to one of the cabbies. "Take me to the railway station."

The cabbie didn't stir.

"I'm in a hurry," Mrs Perkins knocked the cabbie's feet off the seat with her parasol. He got to his feet, grumbling.

When they had driven off, Matilda came out from behind the horse.

"I think this young lady's trying to get your attention, Harry," one of the cabbies said. "Or maybe it's your horse she's taken a shine to."

"I want to take a cab to the cemetery," Matilda said blushing.

"Harry's your man, Miss."

Harry got up ready to go.

"Not today," said Matilda.

"When did you have in mind then?"

"Wednesday morning. I'd like you to pick someone up from a house in Albert Street."

"Someone?"

"An old woman who wants to visit the cemetery. If you could come at 10 o'clock."

"And how do I know I won't be wasting my time?" asked Harry suspiciously.

"I'll give you a shilling in advance."

The cabbies all laughed at this. Matilda began to think that it was she who was wasting her time. Harry took pity on her though.

"Okay," he said. "I'll do it. Which house in Albert Street?"

"The very last house."

"All right, young lady. I'll see you on Wednesday morning."

"Don't come to the front of the house," said Matilda. "Go round the back and wait."

Matilda gave Harry a shilling and hurried away so she didn't have to listen to their jokes.

When Matilda went to look for Po Po on Wednesday morning, she wasn't in the stables or in the garden. The back gate was open and Matilda found her crouched behind the paling fence next door. She was watching the neighbour's chickens pecking at the dusty dry earth. Matilda was about to say that the cabbie would be there any minute when one of the chickens suddenly keeled over and lay motionless in the dirt. Matilda couldn't believe her eyes. It was just like Lizzie had said. Po Po could kill chickens just by looking at them. The old woman chuckled to herself and hobbled over to get the chicken.

She was still laughing when they got back to the stable. She laughed even more when Matilda asked her how she could kill chickens with a glance.

"It's not dead," Po Po said. "It's just sleeping." She twisted the limp bird's neck sharply. "Now it's dead."

She showed Matilda a packet of Chinese herbs that her son had given her to help her sleep. Matilda knew for a fact that Po Po always slept like a log.

"I cook the herbs with some grain,"

explained the old woman. "When the chickens eat the grain, they fall asleep. I should have roast pig to offer to the Hungry Ghosts, but they will have to make do with chicken."

The cabbie came promptly at 10 o'clock. Po Po was as excited as a child going to the fair. She had a canvas bag over her arm containing the chicken as well as grapes and peaches, and she was wearing embroidered red slippers on her tiny feet. Matilda went with her to the back gate. She gave money to Harry and instructed him to drop Po Po at the cemetery and pick her up again at two. Harry looked at the little Chinese woman fearfully.

"I'm not going to the Chinese cemetery," he said. "I've heard they do black magic to bring back the dead.

"That's not true," said Matilda. "They say prayers to their dead relations. It's part of their religion, no different than going to church."

Harry was not convinced. He was ready to give Matilda her money back. Po Po started to wail softly to herself. The Hungry Ghosts would make her life miserable if she didn't go to this ceremony. They would break her vases and make her bean curd go bad.

"What if I come with you and give you an extra half-crown?" Matilda asked. "You don't have to go anywhere near the Chinese part of the cemetery."

Harry reluctantly agreed. Matilda rushed inside to get a bonnet. Lizzie was looking for her. She wanted someone to help wind knitting yarn. Matilda ignored her, hurried to the back gate and clambered into the carriage. Harry flicked his whip and they were away, leaving Lizzie standing at the gate open-mouthed.

Matilda could count on one hand the number of times she'd been in a carriage. Every time, it had been to the cemetery. Her first carriage ride was to her mother's funeral, though she couldn't remember it. Her last carriage ride had been when her father died.

Harry dropped them outside the cemetery, promising to come back at two. With Matilda supporting her on one side and the lion's head walking stick on the other, Po Po shuffled slowly and painfully toward the smell of smoke and roasting meat. The gravestones changed from those with angels, crosses and English words to simple gravestones with Chinese characters on them.

It looked like the entire Chinese population of Ballarat was gathered there. Matilda recognised some of them—the paper cutter and the cook from the Golden Phoenix, the kitemaker and the temple guard. They nodded politely. Everyone else stared. Matilda and Po Po were the only women there, Matilda was the only non-Chinese.

Everyone was gathered around a big fire over which three pigs were roasting. Spread on the ground in front of the fire, were other offerings—piles of fruit, pots of tea, bowls of noodles. Po Po added her fruit and the limp chicken to the offerings. The air was thick with the scent of burning incense. Firecrackers were let off. Gongs and cymbals clashed. The noise was enough to wake the dead, which, Matilda realised, was probably what it was supposed to do. A man in a coloured gown said some words and the other people chanted in reply. Then they all knelt down and prayed, each person saying his own prayer. The noise was a babble. The prayers went on for some time.

"The ghosts have had their fill now," explained the temple guard, once the prayers were over. "Now we can eat."

Slices of meat were cut from the roasting pigs and everyone ate. Matilda had stayed at a distance during the prayers, but her friends invited her to join them. She sat on the grass, ate pork and noodles using chopsticks and drank tea. Other Chinese who she didn't know were amazed when they heard her speak in their language.

"You must be very clever," said one old man. "Your pronunciation is terrible, but I'd heard that Big Noses were all too stupid to learn Chinese."

The afternoon passed very pleasantly, until

Feast for the Ancestors 87

a dozen or more Australian youths suddenly appeared from nowhere. They kicked over the incense burners and trampled the picnic. They picked up fruit and threw it at the Chinese. They smashed teapots and cups. Matilda went to help Po Po who was struggling to get to her feet. One boy saw Matilda and shouted at her, calling her names—traitor and Chinese-lover. Someone threw a peach at her. The youths became more violent and started punching anyone who tried to resist them. Someone pulled out a knife and cut off a Chinese man's pigtail. Matilda knew that without the pigtail, the man would not be able to return to China. The other Chinese all ran in fear.

A man in a suit ran up and grabbed Matilda by the arm. He gathered up Po Po and hurried them to a carriage. It was Uncle William.

"Your aunt sent me out to look for you. I guessed you would be here."

"What was that all about?" asked Matilda as they rode away. "Why did those men attack the Chinese?"

"It's because of the gold find," Uncle William explained. "The Australian diggers resent the Chinese having so much gold. It's not the end of the trouble."

When they got home, Henry was outside the gate with his new ornithopter in his arms. Aunt Philadelphia came out onto the verandah wearing a thunderous frown. Henry took one look at her and decided he didn't want to visit after all. He turned away from the gate.

Inside the house, Matilda had to listen to a lecture on responsibility and proper Christian behaviour. Her aunt had a whole list of things for her to do as punishment. Learning long sections of the Bible by heart formed a large part of it. Aunt Philadelphia was just listing the extra chores she would have to do every day, when a crash and the sound of breaking glass came from the front of the house. The babies started crying. Everyone rushed to the girls' room. The window was broken. On the floor between the babies' cots was a brick with "Chinese-lover" scrawled on it in very bad handwriting.

Matilda rushed to the door and out into the street. She could see someone running toward the diggings. She shouted at the top of her voice "Stop that man!" though there didn't seem to be anyone around to hear her. She ran as hard as she could, holding up her skirts without caring who saw her legs. She knew she would never be able to catch the man but she was so angry she had to do something. Then she saw Henry bending down over his ornithopter.

"Henry," she yelled. "Stop him!" though she knew he wasn't the sort of boy who could attack criminals with his bare hands. As usual, Henry didn't seem to hear Matilda. The fleeing man was getting away, disappearing in the uneven ground of the diggings.

Then Matilda saw the ornithopter take off. It lifted two metres in the air and swooped off in the direction of the fleeing man. He heard the loud whirring noise and turned back to see the strange contraption heading toward him. The machine was flying far too slowly to ever catch up with him, but the man didn't know that. He wasn't looking where he was going. His foot slipped and he fell, toppling down a half-dug mine shaft. The ornithopter crashed into a slag heap.

"Oh, Henry," gasped Matilda as they both ran to the hole. "One of your machines has accidentally done something useful."

"Well now, what makes you think it was an accident?" Henry asked.

They peered down the mine shaft at the man who was clutching his twisted ankle. He was still down the hole when Uncle William came with the constable to arrest him.

That night, the Australian miners jumped the Chinese claim where the gold had been found. The Chinese diggers were driven off. Rocks were thrown, shots were fired. Someone sent for Uncle William to care for the wounded.

It was nearly midnight and the house was quiet at last. Aunt Philadelphia, Betsy, Lizzie and Po Po were all finally in bed. Matilda looked in at the sleeping babies. Her blood ran cold when she thought of how close they had come to being injured.

Uncle William came home, exhausted. Matilda got him some supper and made a pot of Chinese tea. He told her that one Chinese had been killed and a dozen badly injured. The claim jump had been successful. The new gold find belonged to Australians now.

"But surely they won't be able to keep it," said Matilda. "They didn't find it. The Chinese miners can go to court and demand that it's returned to them, can't they?"

Uncle William shook his head. "The Chinese cannot use Australian courts," he said. "The law of this land does not act for them."

"But that's not fair," said Matilda. "They have to go to jail if they do something wrong. They paid licence fees that allow them to mine."

Uncle William shrugged and sipped his tea. Matilda went to her room, but not to sleep.

Instead, she went to her writing desk and took out a clean sheet of paper. She addressed it to the editor of the *Star*. This is what she wrote:

> Dear Sir,
> It is with feelings of greatest anger that I write to protest about the senseless act committed tonight at my home. My baby sisters came near to being injured by a brick thrown through a window. Innocent children are at risk when people let hate grow in their hearts.
> My stepfather also tells me that a Chinese man was shot dead as Australian miners jumped his claim. If a Chinese had taken an Australian claim, it would rightly be called theft and the man would be in jail or more likely hanged. Instead, the thieves celebrate openly and no-one is arrested for this murder.
> As Christians, we should be ashamed that such injustice goes unpunished in our town.
> Yours sincerely,

Matilda put down her pen and thought for a moment. Then she picked up the pen and signed the letter Matilda Mabel Maud Chow Mong.